GOOD EURYDICE

GOOD EURYDICE

POEMS

ANDREW HALEY

OTIS NEBULA PRESS
SALT LAKE CITY
MMXI

© 2011 by Andrew Haley
ISBN 978-0-9849989-0-6
Printed in the United States of America

Oh, tourist
Is this how this country is going to answer you

And your immodest demands for a different world

—*Elizabeth Bishop*

CONTENTS

PARIS – HONG KONG
KAOHSIUNG
BANGKOK – SYDNEY

Hotel Gay Lussac	11
Couldn't Tear	12
Fortunato	13
A L'ancienne	14
Trieste	15
Balkanized	16
For Chagall	17
St Petersburg Dream Poem	18
Colorosoleum	19
Rainstorm Outside Omsk	20
Antichrist	21
Emei Shan	22
Emei Shan II	23
On Emei Shan Thinking of Li Po	24
The Famous Grouch	25
To a Book	26
Tropic	27
Christmas	28
Mercy	29
Antebellum	30
Invasive	31
Atlantis	32
Multitudes	33
Hang Chow Hotel	34
Tanah Rata	35
Poem for Elena	36
Poem Consigned to Infinity	37
Kings Cross	38
Sydney	39

SALT LAKE CITY

Glad	43
After Li Po	44
Politic	45
Poem for Larry on His Birthday	50
Pangenesis	51
Meow	52
Three Cha'an Poems	53
Sacre du printemps	54
Ave Maria	55
Roses	56
Depart XIII	57
Internationale	58
Russia House #2	61

BUENOS AIRES

In Valparaiso	65
Poem for Ginsberg	66
Letter Without Destination	67
Japanese Poem	68
Poem for David Hockney	69
Why I Wish I Was a Painter	70
Labyrinths	71
23/11/2004 22:36 Buenos Aires	72
Puzzle	73
Heroes	74
Orpheus	75
Epistle	76
Letter to Two Thousand and Five	77
Poem in the Campo	79
Rebuttal	80
Dear America	81
Poem to Get Started	82
New	85
Morning	92

PARIS – HONG KONG
KAOHSIUNG
BANGKOK – SYDNEY

HOTEL GAY LUSSAC

Enormous shadows slide
over the enormous countryside

      WHITE
clouds
    quit
        ~~Burgundian~~   quit Burgundy

    presse windowboxes cold

dark socks   WHITE
          socks
                for sweet
                      tiny
                            toes

    on the sill
            out shopping

in a sunken mall

    Bloom Plúmb Soon
    enormously

COULDN'T TEAR

Cute and cool the swimmers swim
benign I never worry
at the whiskers of our midnight bed
a car goes zoom and I go zoom

Blue streets yellow
and if they lime I lime
there is no cause
besides all of them

The liquefaction of a hill
means you say hello
and offer me a plate of squid
and a red car on a green street
proves the Atomic Energy Commission
murdered grandma's thoroughbred

Wild mustangs
gunned in Box Canyon
wore a wild coat
galloped in a swell
of fiery sand

FORTUNATO

Magnanimous as orchards
the green interior
gives sea a cool noon

Repose
as on a boat
to nowhere
~~on~~ no particular day
bountiful with circumstance
among a school of fish
that remain unnamed
by the ossuary of the shore

Fine soil grows cherries and a feline friend

A street rises to the green shade in a new chemise

In darkness gold gathers the light to it

Happy   day   light   gives
     the   gold
            away

A L'ANCIENNE

Here is the Moor gate
which opened to horror and quick disaster
moist mortar here cranked by footmen, ruined
on orders of Louis Quatorze

Here nets are hauled
bright with anchovy
keels plowed white rich over green
coasting the deep blue

Here Greek ships, low on water, craving olives
passed under cliff edge
made bright where rocks among cypress
alit with southerly sun

Here where the headland lowers
they dubbed it Victory
near where Prince Albert looms
over the bandstand with a cigar

TRIESTE

Even you in the sequined or is it snakeskin blue shoes
tossed over the hood of a European car
Even you just ahead above shoulders in the circuit of breakers
Even you interrupting me about Croatia
Even suspended aloft in the mild morning yellow robed buffoon
flaming Saxon Jesus Christ with your Nintendo
Even you spooning wasabi in the Los Angeles hotel
Even you Your Excellency in Trieste for a week without an escort
Even you on leave en route to Palestine before your sex change
This is not a flood of energy circling democratically
or is it this is not the jumpinjackflash you wished were
revisiting Padova for the frescoes
Does Giotto count as drama swearing in Triestino
Cristo en merda you nun's cunt colored exile
Exhale – weirdness has nothing on anchovy sandwiches

joy joy joy joy : joy joy joy joy – dong

Even you father crapping in the stall of the stazione municipal
Even you should love the turtles get a job
Go to Italy work is overrated
The hotdog guy sold hotdogs through the hurricane
My brain, is op, to no, godo, swicting letsers
around where I don't put them even you even
Jesus isn't that the point
Be the pope be the antipope
Visit Venice in a doctor's mask and fuck the courtesans
Fill the mules with rats and fire them over the wall
Fill the car with ether and drive for miles

Balloons
        Streetlight on the green canal
scattering white ~~musi~~coins
        for everybody
This is a poem for everybody

BALKANIZED

Nor in the too quiet of the courtyard
moony-blue boughs
slope-headed moon
        among
                switch
                        -ed chan
                              -els
                                      BOO!
should'st thou forget
galloping into the soonest hotel

no he didn't love you in mono either

nor the flatiron swan length extending noonfirst
along her sunned mat   on the roof pool of the Hotel Byzantium
nor lies about a toothbrush
      applause = applesauce

why these unmoorings soonest mended later moor
hollow to hollow
love to loved

old prayer/rebellion : candle will
               NOT
            go out
              WE
            will
          not go out

FOR CHAGALL

An angel on roller skates
not given over to wood gilt
wit's cut – yet

    angel is attention
held   moment
    this is my sacristy
    this is *every* body's pietà
Captain Ludicrous is
not Ludwig is anyway
Ludwig in red hose

You should have been there
with us that day round
the chowder kettle

That night in the square
where held wet
where a long rose
in wit's place

Who walked in
Who shook
everybody's hand
all in black &
roman
        nosed
wood sky painted with the stars
military band in the wet square
give up   give music
a star worth
gazing
for

Held   violet sky
after rain
not an angel an angel
these are Kraków poems

ST PETERSBURG DREAM POEM

cOlo	coOO	coOl	OsoO
OOOR	OloO	Ooor	Colo
OSOO	rOos	oOsO	roso
cOolor	OOo	Oo	Ocol
OoosO			oOro
oO			OsoO

COLOROSOLEUM

Red hole where cool rose
Golden ossuary
Cut from stone
Cool hole cut for bones
In light lit white
Red on rose

RAINSTORM OUTSIDE OMSK

for Mouse

John-baring his bum on the ricket-
Y trellis, A rued.
Rude A coming from a fight w/ Bunny
Consternated arsewards his frustration.
Nothing; to no laudation.
And there sat hippopotamus A
Beside his rat,
And ruefully his ruicide commat.

ANTICHRIST

I'm the boy whose passport wouldn't fit on Earth.
I'm a raided factory making nothing dangerous.
I'm a museum of odes, a bust open zoo.
I'm the alien in stripes who goes on pissing.
I'm the wall of feces on this train.
I'm a sink drank, a spat down well, an estuary.
I am the Finsky Zaliv.
I'm Lenin's eye. My vision is formaldehyde.
I'm a moon-white corpse in a mid-sized stream.
I'm a carp at an amusement park.
I live under the swings.
I plod around the school testing windows.
I feed on tight young bodies with my eyes.
My breath is gasoline. My farts can crack Formica.
I live in Lake Baikal on sandwiches.
These are my human dreams.

EMEI SHAN

```
                S
               U N
             O N A N
           M U T I S
          E     A     R
         M       L       E
          E     D     E
           R   T   S
```
SLOW CURVE OF DARK JADE STREAM

EMEI SHAN II

```
      SUN
     OVER
  M    N    I
   O    T    N
     U    A    S
```

ON EMEI SHAN THINKING OF LI PO

Leaves shake like dragonflies on Emei Shan
Plunging waters of the white stream
Carve a gulf in rock shaggy with bamboo
The temple of Puxian roars with tourists' cries
Children pound the sacred bell
On the Monkey Mountain trail tourists bunch
Around one-eyed monkey amputees
They snarl, eating litter, and leap from path to tree
At Qingying taped music plays in the Buddhist store
Stopping for Blue Sword Beer at the summit of red stairs
Elena stares into the misty flattened reaches
Of mountains and rivers without end
Li Po, be happy you are dead

THE FAMOUS GROUCH

Sun in octopus of cyclone is the king of pearls
Stone of chance a throw will never kill
Pearl edifice reflected
In IM Pei's mood mirror
And the gem of Star Ferry in the lapping jade
Mean voilà amie nous sommes au-delà
I second your hooray – I second the space elevator
Ribbons taught with sleds accelerating from the world's sledge
Let's ride – I want a bicycle that isn't spelled right
I want a soft landing, cheap scotch, no cockroach eggs
This is love; where the romance over Hong Kong let's me breathe
That isn't love; is needlework @ St. John's, or planks for kiddies
Drawn across the rattan; is prayer for self-salvation
Ice cream ad on the MTR : chocolate-vanilla yin and yang
Diane Lane tripping on the mind, movie star priest
Chance of mood. You are a jewel. You make me
Heavier   I   thank   you   Love   World

TO A BOOK

Wizards branch   and a dull window pangs
Thread of love   tight in dreaming   threat
Of hodgepodge   swirl of blur-blind day thoughts
Vs. octopus green of cool nocturne etc.
A night book   should be different   etc.
In the afternoon I do not love you
In bright hours when pupils ache I do not love you
The athletic longing   the quiet venomous disgust
Dream flaps into the world on stubby wings
Out of an abandoned quarter   tears reopens
Flies out of this abandoned quarter   odd and broken
Syncope : unloved unloved unloved unloved

TROPIC

Mist plays lies
Hiding tropical shimmy
Of late November's shine
Mocktyphoons, rather,
Gloucesters. Palms
With Gloucester fog.
But jacket whipping
Motorscooter's lee
I'm warm and empty
Tables fill the Chinese rooms.

CHRISTMAS

Moose picks its scabs and bleed
Mormons cruise through wet on wheels
You sulk in damp sheets and Puli rains
Thin-stalked betel nut shag their heads in gloom

MERCY

Doc ships emptiness to new strands
Legions love it
They play rondels on brown bassoons

I'm a horse in prison
I'm a jewel
I stay drunk for reason

You find hairs where the crime was
She's in a bag she doesn't mind
Leaf   Dune   Drudgery

Poor King Faisal
breaks his heart and doesn't know
now is the winter
and the sun
shines

ANTEBELLUM

Morning packing for Maolin
Peanut butter wok and trout
They'll be in Baghdad in 2–4 days
We'll be home Monday by 2 PM
Unimpeded, we'll drop in

Sick I wrote this down
Sick I told you
Sick I told anyone

INVASIVE

1

My paranoia knows no bounds. My hyperawareness undrapes them all. Naked conspiracies pepper the Earth. I see the conspiracy between the farting oxen and the cranes. I see the conspiracy between the leaves and the green. Between the zither and the qin. Between the wharves and the worlds of cartoons.

2

Confluences and congruities, likeness swelling into likeness, benzene swimming into flame, a topology of asterisks, a whorl of glints-on-glass, dimes at the bottom of a pool; starry, starry.

ATLANTIS

Utopic   night soot   again
A cigarette again   night wash hanging
Mildewed over night lane
Cinched into slits between bricks
Paved   blue neon slumbering on greasy tiles
Fan's loose axel digs into its wobble
I am too tired for boredom but I am bored
He didn't die and then he died –
The story of the Chinese Icarus
Ocean surrounds us
Heat brings us nearer the sea nearer to our
Sweltering in rooms with greasy floors
Bamboo mats with mold in the partitions
Our fancy is a tart – our fancy comes home
Every other night a swabby's girl
Inches up the stairs out of the dawn's
Stain
With newer nowhere to hang our fits on
Aero : contours of shade across a broken surface
Cubes of habitation sprawling into the suburbia of
Generations – cockroach virility, the virility
Of chlorine, hallowed nectar of dust threaded in
There is no sin in God's perfect sinking . . .
Las Vegas – our sinking heart –
No   Where

MULTITUDES

for Elena

Wake to sun on white plaster
In a whorl of fan-cooled air
You sleep beside me, face down
Golden legs from white blanket
Lips swollen with sleep

HANG CHOW HOTEL

Hot coffee sweetened with canned milk
Voice from America in the traffic sound
Old sailor smiling this morning
Over red tea (black in ships' holds only
Sun hot in my outstretched hand
Monsoon afternoon don't need a weatherman
Bright blue late morning old Penang

TANAH RATA

Dawn prayer's triple echo
Cold valley wet
With last night's rain

POEM FOR ELENA

Sun on the pebbled wall of the waterfall
Pink blossom behind your ear behind you
The twisting branch heavy with pink flowers

POEM CONSIGNED TO INFINITY

White walls over the salinated pale
Half sea never once loved more
My heart opens a channel to my eyes
My eyes are instruments of God
Exercise effortless sun everywhere
White walls and a white sky everywhere
Things pale in the still halo
Half sea the afterbirth of a closed
Time a packet white under pale crust
Morning noon afternoon without shadow
New day permanency the interrupture
Of a burp of a new need flying
Everywhere the white sun balances

KINGS CROSS

White.
Winter.
Three o'clock water slashed. Nonaggression is best.
Snow at noon, a lettered
Arrow of sun.
I can tell you that.
You read winter words to a priest on a bunk bed.
My hands read the infrared wall. They say:
everything everything.
Moving backwards.
I declined the crucifix. There was no white divan.
Hobos and skateboarders. The women here say
fuck every chance they get.
Some women smile. Some launder.
I am thinking about a can of engine oil
in my father's garage.
Dickinson would hate that.
      can – engine oil –
      father's garage
A cloud stuns me. A fountain shows everyone their faces.
White hulls
too bright
to see.

SYDNEY

Last hours
Danae frantically packing
wind bounce of blinds and the elevated
train making its long turn
celestial city higher than clouds
that should be
        celestial
        city higher than clouds
clouds intermixed in the gleaming stalks
the faint crisscross of cranes
there are no last hours
dog yapping in the arbor
sun shines in on the leather sofa
color of my skin
Danae zipping re-zipping
socks in their spot among things
wind stirs
in the bright apartment
winter leaves on the public stairs
slap of anger, taut straps
"now"
there is no last hour

Morning   September second two thousand three
city colossal in sunlight
mortar and mortar
brick to brick
salutation of ochre and brown
salutation of black windows and
morning sky ashen nearer the ground
sun comes in at angles
warming patches of the floor, my shoulder
slap of shower water on the shower floor
sound of distant spoons
dropped in a drawer
articles cinched against foam
things wound in their restraints
of dirty clothes/dirty clothes

stuffed in plastic/plastic
in nylon
ibises honk and holler
                              gliding
over trees
flying foxes warm their wings
upside down

Morning hours open sun's full day
noon is northerly
the big towers curve their masked tops
into the shadows that borrow
the shadows of trees
the park is dark
sun tinsels and statics
in the gothic arch
of the bridge's boughs
its pointillism shreds
the permanent wall
idle touchups with a table saw

Sunpatch grows   warmth spreads over
tea steam in the shadow of the rattling fridge
last night the neon tops were
         RED   BLUE
stars in their crazy new order over all
now the big star offers its yellow to metropolis
metropolis obliges with an ochre bough

SALT LAKE CITY

GLAD

to be from way out west
so I can say re Coalville
yeah that's the next town up
towards Wyoming and mean it
and know it.

And though Peter Covino
has such nicely pressed shirts
and always a sharp haircut
last night we went up Millcreek
Canyon and broke branches
with our hands and the help
of stream smooth granite boulders.

Pine smells good
when it burns.
Light fell over
red aspen leaves
and the dirt needed
no addendum.

Ate in the dark with a folding knife
blackened chilies corn and steaks
tasting of fall and pine smoke and
happiness is happiness.

AFTER LI PO

Noon prisms
pale
on maple
among
patterns of sun

November's
winter clarity

Branches without
leaf pattern
interfold
winter patterns

Sun through high
clouds
floating heavy
with tomorrow's
snow

POLITIC

What you must bear, you will.
—James Schuyler

Sorrow governs sorrow
There is no liege there
        The tentacles of power extended to the West
Coils of rhetoric maneuvered in November brown
Dreams of lovers torn apart by nature weigh
the kitchen down
        How far?
Mind
The dogs howl
In the basement the puppy learns to squeal
        from the basset hound
Sticks across the view from a dirty window
Backlit cottonwoods intercept bruised clouds
Hanging in the sky like MRIs
        All we need is love

Squash and an unfrozen loaf
share the granite tabletop with me
A week old cake in blue polyurethane
One slice of bread– the heal
Bucket of Darigold sour cream with two cookies left inside

These domesticities don't elevate the mood
the way sudden parting of cloud admits
a torrent of sunshine
blinding the screen in a flurry of illuminated dust
        I call them illumined
        quoth Berliner #9

Sitting on the floor last night I watched a show about Treblinka
thought –   write a poem
about the Germanness of killing in small quarters,
        organization . . .
                thought again – don't do that

Later, hearing of the waitress with renal failure
sister in law covering her shifts
tried to remember Creeley's poem
        what should not have to be said…
The puppy squeals out of sympathy

Sorrow governs sorrow
It is an overlapping land
A republic with its own laws
and a quiet apparatus
for security

Black coffee in my cup—

        The
      Oxford Hotel
        Denver

Thinking of Sundin
lost in Denver lost to Salt Lake lost in the alley of talent
Cervantes' house
across from that Laundromat
down a backstreet in Madrid

The winter sun is distant
blooming over a field of desert flowers
far from here where enlightened children pick
red berries from a coffee bush
reeling from the whip
of their enlightened poverty
that drains the mucus out of sorrow
to reveal a bright winter pain
scorching the amazing plants
growing in their clime

        How far?
        How unreal?

Yellow, fanged snakes tear apart a girl
in my morning dreams
        a girl
whose hot brown body I made love
the tenor of a tired day
whose hot brown body made me love
the squalor of a Californian motel
and our joy was the gift we gave
long ago in the sunny solitude
of happiness
        unreal

Standing paunched, face sheared, in my mid-November living room
thought – how would I know?
Love for old lovers
held
        deep in a private heart
        deeper than the drudgery of squabble
place where the angels who greet us in the tunnel of our death abide

But love
        without sympathy?
        sympathy
neutered by the crystalline
            facts
        of this republic
        burying the possibility
        of a ubiquitous hello

How would I know?
I could not help? I could not pity when sorrow broke her
What is this distance?
Why are we cold?
Why use simile?

Sorrow governs sorrow
It is a republic of the mind
The praetorian guards hang their apparatus
on our sagging mood

The soft covers
of cold things
cover a table
in November

Empty bottle
Empty kettle
The last cold sips
of coffee

Where is that democratic joy
I envisioned eleven years ago
elevating one another
without irony or pretence
sharing
        happily
                our common joy?
Where is the democracy of happiness
I wandered out for and wandered back again
and could not find
in the cold cage of this republic?

My body begins to sag
The bodies of my compatriots
too begin the slow parade
towards the wonderland
of hidden angels
all these years
weighing down our hearts

My heart is heavy with happiness
I carry the unrealities of bliss
anchovies and train rides
stupefied by wonder
coasts and mornings
fantastic bodies undressing
in the cathedral of two
anonymities sharing anonymity
love sharing love and secrets
snowflakes and the affection

of dead dogs whose greasy collars
smell
across the cage of present fact
hiding in a dog house while divorce
unwound a garden of rusting toys
the clear dementia of August's purple sky
July wonderland running
briar and rhubarb
walking all night over dry hills
through scrub oak and straw
aurora borealis we thought was nuclear war
the night the moose visited our wickiup

"Leave this behind   Walk into the world

Leave this?   and go alone into the republic?
It is my map to the democracy that gives me shape
It is the instant of my faith
in joy and common
prisms fill November's room

POEM FOR LARRY ON HIS BIRTHDAY

You drank gin
like the boys in fifties helicopters
drank gin.
You're giving up gin.

Gertrude Stein believed in sentences.
Your son says God's a mechanical engineer.

You dug sunken submarines out of fathoms of mire
and made an inelegant suit
for inelegant man to land
on the elegant moon.

Snow is falling.
It's your birthday.

I'm drinking gin doubled over
from cold and the bare black
branches are cropped with white tops
that earlier obscured the green

echoes of fireworks. Larry,
what can young men say to old men?
Thanks, Godspeed? Godspeed, into the darkness?

What can a young man like me, broke, shivering, give
a man who has come happily at last

to the end of necessity? Except
though not tonight
I'll follow you friend
into the elegant quiet of quiet snow.

PANGENESIS

My Herculean father
in asymmetry, my eye slopes
as your eye slopes. We're
too lecherous though you're
overweighed by work, who
escaped work into the burden
of necessity. I'm rich in the starvation
you brokered out of into wealth
that hangs its polyps of happy
leisure over me. I'm not hopeless.
I correct you. ~~We are of a Kind.~~
= Love. And a poem that
        cannot be written yet.

MEOW

The cat's a genius & still
Bukowski's dead.
He sits on the porch as elegant as Ramses.
Someone's always gonna let him in.

Winter now
he's twice his size & checks
behind the drapes we draw
against the cold panes
above the radiator
in the bay where Danae's
succulent squats
opaque in the electric light.

Cat stalks
testing his claws on wool cushions
slinking into the cracks into I don't know where
eager for new dusts
rolling in the pile of Elena's shoes
each stroke of winter coat hungrier than I.

THREE CHA'AN POEMS

I
Rain-wrenched from April boughs,
scattered blossoms disarray the ground.

II
Quick-necked, a full-bodied bird
drops torn, wet blossoms from its beak.

III
Shadows dull the sun, then undull
this white chaos of illuminated boughs.

SACRE DU PRINTEMPS

After the rain,
dripping blossoms
sag to the top of the grass.

AVE MARIA

for Tamrika

There are things to tell you. They wear dusty masks wet with the pulp of my inner chaos. I drove a long way once. I went to a city with two towers and three moons. That's the inside I'm talking about.

When we do this we are gambling. While I sit here the neighbors are calling their dog fucker. I think I'm dumb. Other times I think I'm very smart. Then usually I read something.

You are the most beautiful person I have ever known.

I'm not talking about the things they say in magazines. When I look into your almond eyes I see the Kandahar of my happiness. For their sake I'll say Los Angeles. For your sake I'll say that you and I believe in forces. For somebody else we know I'll tell you what I mean.

Everybody dies. Five-foot names dipping from the smog of heaven peter out and fret and flicker and throw themselves flat as neon into darkness. We have senses. They tell us who and what and when and where. You get a short time here.

Let's make things that make things go!

In other words you and I like things that make things better later. We don't care about the linoleum of the dry land. We care about black seas and singing on answering machines and one time you called me just to say it snowed. Those are the kinds of things I'm talking about. Or at least they point the way.

I am listening to music and your name has jagged edges that I love. Just for you I love the letter K. And I want to take this opportunity to say thanks (even songs end) for helping me when I didn't know to know.

ROSES

for Elena

which wet hang down to the driveway the color of I don't remember
and even if I knew are nothing compared to wet pink roses with
the headlights off and the leaves wet too of course let's not be stupid
in pursuit of the poetical. I like birds more each day and feed
them the broken crusts of bread instead of sending all that flour
to the landfill even if it does end up splattered white marks of shit
on my folding chair. I hear them coo and curl their feathered
throats and the bush shakes in the evening with five kinds
of song and in the wet night roses and petals and cement and
ground are wet so too the birds are wet in their stooped
positions with their almost human hearts and they are almost
as happy as I was crawling into bed with you drunken as always
my mind full with the sight of wet pink roses and I should
mention they were shaggy and unkempt far from prissy English
roses that don't deserve to be in a poem about you.

DEPART XIII

Summer wrings my heart out
Summer burned into red
shoulders ladders burnt into songs
into children into fennel bursting absolutely
from parched hill I dig stubbornly
and dig over the lintel scraped ready
for primer and my awkward brush and
I am writing about I because you
have left for that white shining ragamuffin
city over bay over balcony over pray
not an Italian painter whose parents
pay his rent or is it your rent now
and the emptiness at nine-fifteen
after a day on the ladder fearing
altitude and the collision sucks
the frayed skin I burnt with spirits
in on the hollow where the kernel
I am missing was before you
dragged it serendipitously west
and left me here shrinking in on myself.
My memories rip disappearances until
you stand above this poem about me
throwing your hips and elbows
around as in the dirty kitchen
we once occupied and drifting
smaller ash shaving shit flake I
vanish into a poem about you.

INTERNATIONALE

for Elena

You hollowed out the world's cities with your ghosts
I watch Moscow in the dark that makes us equals
Matt is in the next room fighting with Lisa – blond,
legs, BMW, jealous of Alexa who I last saw
at Joe Creek the day you left me or we left
each other and here my body hurts in and out

and I'm at the Sherry bottle once again
just like Madrid the ten days after
I put you on a plane to Gatwick and starved
myself fat on fried ham and eggs, Ducados,
absinthe, the view of laundry in the pit of courtyard
the dirty window across the street from Cervantes' house

Where are you? Tramping in Mexico laughing at someone's
jokes in a bar I'd love or hate or are you cozy in Eugene,
smiling at the new life ahead carved down and shining?
Matt just closed the door on Lisa's protests,
as if he thought I didn't know the noise
of love and heart's wrung out sorrow, sore

here from baseball that last day my scabs
like claw marks up an abdomen you touched drunk
in the dark holding me a last night before
sundering this habit of traveling into each
other and our cities and the new flash
of clotheslines and smog – I can't go anywhere

without the ghosts of our fastest year
smoothing hollows in the flattest features
sharing continual sorrow, wondering, regrets
with a future whose face I fall in love with
at the movies. She's young and has a funny
mouth shaped like Tamrika's and Matt Damon

cups her no he doesn't I cupped our memories
in my sore heart in the darkness watching
Moscow and the world flash and Lisa's
angry. I'm not cut out for this. I need
the ready partner at my hip on the road
and I don't want to settle for no road at all.

Why do I miss you? Because you are me
and I am you and we are the same
filthy station in the middle of the afternoon
drunks sleeping on their faces our faces cut
by streetlights in windows on islands in rain
bougainvillea above the walls where Bonaparte was born

and Jason Bourne in that old theatre in Tainan
when we gave up walking for celluloid
through blue volutes of Chinese cigarettes.
Now you're craving a bigger world, a smaller you.
You cut me out to find just what exactly?
Who do you think I am? What cantina, what

palm tree, what Caribbean, what man or
block or club or swirl of a world of shame
or shamelessness or prostituted deranged life
or shattered hope regorging and reshattered,
what tramped brown país of newspaper buses
and cardiac dawns, what tired snow

what evening dragging your knuckles home from work
what old and damp or cut shard or diamond
what island what degradation what dog
or euthanasia what roll of the dice do you think
I wouldn't swallow for you? I'd step over every
country city cop or copse or river or sea.

I'd even sell myself short with a line like that.
You cut me out. My world welcomes me with arms
of sorrow. You are missing. The bricks and
windows of the Soviet tenements shining with
Mercurial light of dawn, the taxis
and metros as peculiar as new cunts,

the fonts of the newspapers and trills of
tongues, the manner of standing
while watching football over beers in Trieste
the smiling gutted pig and all the details
lack you and when I go to them they
smoke in my face and show me their insides

and the sounds of lovers in another room
play out on carpet while my toes knuckle
the hard floor of a basement kitchen where
I'm thinking about you and your fury and the
cruel years we spent loving one another with
pricks and kicks and patiently beheld the world.

RUSSIA HOUSE #2

for Elena

In the morning Moscow magazines
sounding out Cyrillic over currant scented tea –
Listen to these lines – horrible as lace
throw them over a broken chair – not likely!
I need a poem voluptuously sinewed
flexible as a whore or even better

a tart socialite, about nineteen,
a poem I can bend on a dirty bed
in a room with a lamp shade glued
to the ceiling, skull and Leonardo
so I can talk about swimming
with you

in those exotic names of places
even sometimes in real water
sometimes with real waves
where I waved from the water
no I didn't and you
read under the palms and didn't see

or swam out together to the mooring
and climbed into the feathered bow
of an Andaman no it wasn't
long boat under the tropics or not
because it doesn't matter how I think
things were they weren't they were

it's all a feeling I have or haven't
about you
a poem I can slap around and throw
on the bed in your father's room
cause he's in Petersburg where you
and I are supposed to be
or was it Istanbul or Odessa or
bobbing down the coast from Greece

and you
slapped me in the heart and bit my words
while your laundry turns in the dryer
I'm remembering the sound of you

laughing in the living room eating chips
the TV making its incursion in sound bites
half-heard by the cue of a laugh track
and I'm broken
hearted, seared through the cracks
in my heart

singed by a sorrow that cracks
open and shines
from my shattered heart
and you
don't believe in easy
grace or do you

believe in lightness and I'm tethered
to the mooring, to the tide bell
or do I shine and float
above the heavy claims of my body
while you
sink in moods

we crash into like televisions
cars anything with glass the monitor
I shot British style with a .357 from 40 ft.
two colossi drifting under memory's gloom
firing uselessly into the dents
of one another's frowns

it's kaput, it's over
we have separate rendezvous
with a South of brown, vagabond forms
our collection is tied to the tide bell
vanishing into the upsurge of a noon
not blinded/blinded by me/you

BUENOS AIRES

IN VALPARAISO

Neruda, I went to your crooked
house shaped like a boat.
So you were a senator. No one
told me. I'm glad you pinned Whitman
on the door to the helipad
where you planned to park
your helicopter to the stars,
opposite the sparkling whitecaps out
past the half-ring of harbor
where the navy docks their sleek
American vessels, waiting for the next
Iquique. There's a broken kite in the tree
outside the window. Once white,
its balsa cross is snapped. The
wind off Valparaiso's broken lanes
feathers its few frays.
I think you'd leave it there and watch
the weather toy it from your chair
with its green stained ottoman. That
chimney like a too-swollen poem dreamt
by an old man. A place to warm
your jowls and remember tomatoes
and goats and girls and the open road
before they put you in the ground.

POEM FOR GINSBERG

Allen I wish you'd been there
my fingers stink and I had to throw off my old shirt
The birds are out there crying Egypt! Egypt!
and you're down there in the clay.
Those girls while the Devil sang in the
here I go losing it to Mick.
What I want to say is, the birds
are singing over Mendoza while the sun
comes up like it did in gay
Paris the day I worshiped your
grave in proxy: gazing at the dawn
coming home over turnstiles. Do you
like my drunken script in Heaven?
Amigo, if you were as full in the cock
as I for white-pantsed women
you'd ask why I made that trident
and the double-stroked T. Just
to get in the way of saying Man
the Argentines are pretty I mean
pretty. And here I am in the john
of the Hotel Galicia
writing this crappy poem for you.

LETTER WITHOUT DESTINATION

Ice in the bidet, my Eleventh International,
today two words on a newsprint map
made the stars on water of a newsprint photograph
resurrect the dead movie of me and you
in the dead space as creepy as the big cloud
above the puny 30-story building striped black and blue
the palm tree bursting like a star, white plaster cubes
full of families and their tinny conversation – Jalan Besar!
remember? those fits of Coolies, scuze the word,
Singapore's streets couldn't hold. We walked in gutters
holding each other's limbs like leashes, beware
of shit or holes in the autocratic cement. Now
my prostate's boiling over and the test strip of my
Norwegian regina, say it Latin w/ a J, doesn't light
my eyes up like your funny big sunglasses, back
pulpy through bikini straps, or the thought of
your asshole when I used to spread your cheeks
apart while I fucked you bent over an old pillow
in our cold bed, guessing what it felt to feel
me inside you stretching apart those parts I could
get my hands on in a state like that, not
knowing then I'd go a continent apart without
a touch, a feathered thought exchanged across
a room we share. Now I'm digesting oceans,
maps, lures… Here where I'd go on to break the old
swing I stop. You are far from here.

JAPANESE
POEM

Bizet
       shouting
la
       rue
only
       part
I want
       the air
wants
       Saturday
sun
       in
gauze

POEM FOR DAVID HOCKNEY

I am twenty-three years old and I
wear glasses. I am twenty-three years old and I
wear glasses. I
am twenty-six years old for the love of fraternal
affection and I should wear glasses.
This should probably wait
for the twenty-four
red flowered stalks in the white
bucket. This should probably have eyes I
started noticing have black lines, flesh
lines, junctions of flesh and eye ball,
joined for vision/sights of sidewalks
bulging outwards – cupolas, planetariums,
all sides pregnant with possible
future holds for us. Exciting!
I walked down the sidewalk today in Hockney
Vision. I walked down the sidewalk today in
Hockney Vision. I walked down the sidewalk
today and beautiful girls turned around
and everybody's eyes were out
looking for the possibilities.

WHY I WISH I WAS A PAINTER

Aunt Margaret would like me better or anyway might feel compelled
to challenge me to duels or whip me like Rodin wished he could have
whipped Camille or maybe even I could hoist one of her naked Goths
into the scaffolding to pose as Barabbas or whoever dribbled next to XP.

I have a grand plan: I will become David Hockney. If it doesn't work out
I will settle for Eugene Delacroix and walk around the Alto Palermo mall
asking the blond Argentines if they'll pose naked on the barricades howling
Shri Krishna Govinda Hare Murare. Or anyway sketch their pert little noses.

Europe After the Rain. A real Rothko right there on the drywall
where the street-light Rothko would settle if this weren't a poem.
Real poets would come over for dinner and I would seduce them
and pour brandy in their bubble baths and paint them laughing.

I could move to LA and paint swimming pools. I could stay
in Buenos Aires and paint soccer player mullets on our backs
so they would love us and introduce us to Nicole Neumann
who I would paint naked in a triptych just for you.

LABYRINTHS

for Harold Bloom

Here the possible is possible
down
we pick them up &
mullets
their shoes scrape
our hands
touching their breasts
Adolescent girls wear skirts and nobody looks
except the Americans
americans
who everywhere are real
slashed
Mattresses lifted into trees
by real Police who everywhere tuck
their hands into their Kevlar
they are real cops and they have real
muscles under there
about the cats in the grass
stalking the grass
These are words but if you're quick
Burn this!   Kill me!   Wipe the slate clean
and the poem will be gone
eating pasta stalking the grass will still
eat pasta and stalk the grass,
eat pasta and
There are things in there even cats
want to know

Old men fall

People grow

They feel

under their arms

the Real

Bodies are

Placards smashed

because

It is true!
eating pasta
It is true!

The cats
will still
stalk the grass

Buenos Aires

23/11/2004 22:36 BUENOS AIRES

tune
I
heard

Jo
han
es
Brahms

w/
you,
cheat,
at a
drive
in
movie

you
made
me
turn
it
off

this is a poem
for you
Trina

PUZZLE

for Donald Revell

Over there a friend puts friend
into abstract. I am a guy
who likes things real.   My friend
does not slap the bed against the wall
because he is a philosopher
second, and knows I am real.

We have a common friend
who loves your poetry. I know
you love the Wild etc.

There are times for those
three monkeys to be
quiet   listen   look.

HEROES

A.
Not everyone gets to   so you are Moriarty now
and while you're getting back to zero
I get to make the beans and hear   This Song
that Kings and Queens
even after those seven thousand surrenders
to the dull   walls I heard while you busied
and vice versa, friend   now, a table   obit Yesus
but really I mean just that   we can be heroes
this day

M.
and, Captain, do not believe
truck full of Rock n Roll suicide   I forgive the vastness
you cannot drive nor the highway that sticks
to my imagination   these things we forgive only
when we visit them together   My Captain
I forgive you're wonderful I forgive your wonderful
cause of starmen my friend in the kingdom of our motion
when we disregarded weather   two, two

R.
dogs go mad here because of riots that would make you howl
my amigo with an encyclopedia in your throat
there are superteens on the other page and bored police
everywhere the hookers thrill nobody and anarchists vice versa
they all are out there with Che's head on a stake
and ten-pounders that go hump, woof   the shit under foot
of a nation with seams big enough for you to crawl through
there's room enough my friend and we are waiting
for you to come in

ORPHEUS

Your drowned brown form is hoisted from the sea
Blue lips on a brown face I've never seen before
Beaches I once figured were the first of a life
Abandoned now New Year's again Mies van der Rohe's

Pavilion in the rain a broken window a face I can imagine
All your children and fishermen the golden drapes
Sarongs over the faces of what should not have to be said
Bungalows where I thought returns would mean our sharing

Lives boats leaves sandals the sucking sea returns
Floating back into the rearrangement of wood and wires
Christmas summer a girl in winter whose brown body
Cools through the miles to the seasonal change

Equator turning her rain away from me the blue
Over metropolis pulling the small items loose caves shining
From the inside suddenly full new faces washed
Away in sorrow the trees limp and men sit down

Mud flops and wailing breaks itself out of bodies
Drenching the grimaces of the dead and the nurse
Powders a beautiful girl's skin and combs her hair
Wrapping a sheet around and writing on the other side

Number 68 the time the ocean brought her in
I could lift those corpses I could break a door I
Could do nothing in the surge but try to get back
To your brown face smiling in a time that drowned

EPISTLE

Dear God of Buenos Aires
I woke up at five PM to pray.
I love the empanadas. I subsist on them. Your
women blah blah blah. Everyone knows, but
still, staggering. I fear I will be hit by a car.

You should import more vodkas and really
is Bushmills so hard? To please you, I took
a fifth of Quilmes to that park down the lane
between Paraguay and Charcas south of Ortiz
(I thank you for not installing calle Lord Ponsonby)

last night, in the bustle, to avoid the fucking sounds
that make my solitary life a hell, and sat on the wall
with an empanada de pollo and I think it was a liter
since it's still in the fridge and looked at
that pretty church with all its numerology.

Really you should build more. I like the nightclubs too.
I like cheta and bobo in another country.
There was a man on a swing behind me
watching me or your church.
The chains rang as he idled easy there.

LETTER TO TWO THOUSAND AND FIVE

I buried your kin face first in the slop a wave makes.
I heaped the ashes of cadavers between his shoulder blades.
Was 2004 a girl? Lift the tail. See. 2004 can rot,

tits or cock, tits and cock, cock and nipples
burrowed rat deep in the soot. I drop a shovelful
on its back. I bury the tail.

Whatever you are you started in a field of rays—
so many rays they made a field—
so many fields they made a cube of sun

that sat on the streets and softened the rinds.
You started with a blue blossom of sparks
that barely missed the balcony.

I wore a glove of leaves. The sparks and stars
above us in the blue were blue and orange, white, pink
shudders and the morning snuck the birds in

on the backs of leaves, green-gold branches
full of morning, the tables still set, the fruit
soft in the cauldron full of wine, the glasses

ringed with red bottoms, the yellow smile
of the woman I tried to bring to bed
twice my age in the sunshine the linen whiter

than tracks the incoming red-eyes
bled along the sky, bled outward anew
with jets to everywhere as promised.

P.S.

Pray this year fewer children go
where adults end their time here
in the shirt of light.

Pray this year abandon keeps still
takes less of us with it
to the opposite of field.

Pray we sit a little longer
in the sun & together
is a word we ~~know~~ share.

POEM IN THE CAMPO

There are no poems in the campo. There is too much
to do: make boomerangs from driftwood in a meadow
where the bull sniffs the cow and the cow licks the car;
wade out where the trees fell and cast flies you never learned;
bury your shit and watch the alpenglow on the jagged

peak across the Chilean frontier where girls go rafting
and come back with the skin peeling between their bikini straps;
cross bridges in a red Peugeot; jump from bridges; walk dripping
across the grass with a crushed felt hat; cook trout in foil;
live on fire roasted potatoes when there's no fish; row.

You can't row in libraries. You can't ejaculate on pebbles.
You can't float face first in crystalline transparency
seeing the rocks come up before they reach you;
seeing the wires of the fallen bridge and when
you come up the golden shoulders of the girls on the shore.

REBUTTAL

There are pains, good doctor. I worry. Even the bluebird worries.
Then I lie across my roommate's bed under the stars.
I can see them through the basil. Above the light
of Buenos Aires they are faint. From my bed
I see only the sun shining on a white wall.
I see much more from my friend's bed.
He is in Patagonia. You should know
how short life is
because you know everything.
I was going to write you a poem.
Instead I am going to lie here with you
and listen to Daniel Barenboim play Bach's prelude in C major.

DEAR AMERICA

your photos made me nauseous
Hunter Thompson's dead

He stomped Terra
the venal, violent side of your face

portrayed from every angle
on pornographic valentines

I will never go back to you
the boys in that shot are men

but their suits don't fit
I prefer my old friend's scowl

the target over the heart
white paper

where the guns point
where the accidents happen

we never forgive
Give me a home where the buffalo roam and

it was on the edge of the desert when the
high water mark   where the surge

My allegiance to the good sprained earth
where the sun

where red towers
Home is where the heart is

POEM TO GET STARTED

There was a way inside the station
I knew once as a kid
Climb up on the dumpster lid
Bathroom where I learned
The brown soap foam hardened
Human nature is like that
We don't need these damned words
Right is right

When I ran away
Dad pulled over
Said Gary Bishop
Hammer and pentagram
And ever after
Star in circle, upside
Down meant innocence
Under the hammer
But let's be clear
Innocence is the eye
I stuck a wire through
Following the thrill
Of inborn
Fascination, something
Sick I guess most of you
Would say but I don't
Care anymore for diagnoses
Tim is over lord
Tim is a mad jumble of heaping planes
A thoroughfare for the electric
Dream storm vulcanized hallucination

I packed a blue bag with my name sewn in white letters
I got fat on hamburgers
Lingering past dark
Walking mercury light suburban parking strip
Fourth grade easily a hundred
If measured in frustration, loneliness, sorrow
And why not? does it matter

What hours log, doesn't it matter
What the animal
Keens, the registry of the howl?

You turn to pornography
You turn to what they give you
You turn to packets of ketchup and a plastic tray
The color of an amusement park outside Chernobyl
You turn to dirty broken-ankle fields
You mock the new girl with yellow curls for scabies
Fat poor with a pretty face god save you
You get mocked, accessory to hockey mask white trash heavy metal
Accused of heresy in the pea gravel heart
Of fifth sixth seventh grade chain link Marine Corps
You turn to fifty-cent carbonation
You turn to the lure of words whose referents when seen
Vaguely disturb you
You turn to a group of individuals with dull, neo-Nazi
Sympathies you hate, who turn into Buddhists
You hate, who transform miraculously into full blood
Cheyenne you hate and mosques are torn apart
By Hindus in an article on the back of a door
Vaguer yearnings are ignored
One day, without meaning to, you tear somebody's braces out

There is a park
Where you throw Chinese stars
And one day somebody accosts you with a skateboard
And another day, somebody bloodies your nose
And one day you stab a bully in the gut with a piece of wood
And the blood comes out because you have a mother
And sisters
And they know how to get the blood out

There comes the day you wake in the dust watching motes in the light
Knowing
Their sunder and the permanent break
Understanding in the flux of the morning
The arc of foibles
The passage of the vaguely good along the arc of pain

Hours with you in my arms letting the wet
Through to my shoulder, knowing the animal
Smart, knowing the cold
Absolute
Tar paper we nailed not knowing how
Melting in our gloves under the noon
August of skies lashed to a white chair at the bottom of the pool
Lighting my arms on fire with kerosene
My human machine
Hurt hurt hurt
I fucked my joy out with my hands
I fucked my joy out with anybody's hands
I learned the neat opiate trick of sleep
And I will go there
Whenever
It comes around

This is not autobiography
This is a poem for Laurel
Asleep on the couch
Dreaming of easiness

It isn't
The way
It isn't the way
I have to let you know, Laurel,
With your body so particular it has its own thousand-letter definition
For a pattern of jolts and jerks, a way of language, the moving,
Systematic methodology
Of habit, circumstance, memory, genetics, immediate need
There is no word nuanced enough to mutter

I see nothing
In our way
Of codes and vain systems
I am turning back now to the brute animal God

NEW

I know the sorrow
of a moon in orbit
shining the dead face
of reflection down
on a planet lit with trees
turned the dull
color of deserts
botanists point out
are shining in the winters
with small desert flowers
and the roofs of parking garages
covered with the yellow wings
of butterflies
that make the long voyage of oceans
and the Pan-American road along the ocean
I imagine blue as my highway
in their desert dull as my own

There are times
we go home
to a broken home
and shelve regret
in the place regrets go

I have the habit of returning
from decayed municipalities

Call them rotten cities
kiosk zoos of the five mile kind
those zones of human living
among human
called metropolis

I sit on rooftops
I climb dangerous ladders to rooftops
I climb through skylights to find
the overturned stars
sprawling angle to angle

slit up the middle
with avenues
whose light overpours
into the black trapezoids
of public spaces

I wanted the magnanimous
coming together
of separate lives
no watershed
the parting of waters
that brings negatives together
the thrash of sound
the flesh fish
the whale of word
the huge time of love
in a diamond glass
a weed glass
a transparent bowl
the size of mars

Does that matter
to the flesh
you feel
on the underside
of your heart

Does that weigh
in the decisions you make
about skateboards
and tangerines

Or is the flesh too
tired
to sear

I hate this pattern
I kill the question
I annul the life that drags
its wounds

over the earth
to hibernate
in our entwining

There was a house we shared
in a mutual mooring
that took us years
away from the broken séance
of teenaged riding in cars
surfing rooftop starlight

Hours on the carpet
petting the sun
in the crumbs
between polyester

A door that swung
back when you kicked it

I want my boomerang
I want my years back
fleshed to the full brood
nicked in the heart
with the sucker punch of love

Love in a zone
tossed over telling
the zones where
crossed-hearted
stars crossed none
and hours spilled
in the earth
along the trail
towards the grail
of black black

How I hate
to burden
the onward lurch
of meadow metal

Our lives
wear out
then cease

In the interim
Bach's prelude
in a flat major
never dulls

Returning
in the autumn
afternoon
mid-May
dolled up
from the night
before
the thought of you
possesses me
in the dark
the thought
of body
the body thought
out under hands
pierced originally
in trust

First sober abandon
to the wild
of new interiors

A space you said
hollow in your hollow

Cars crashed along beaches
night in the sand
raining hours
sea lions call
across dunes

Over ocean
a way before
peters out
in Minorca
leveling the
entropy
of separated caresses
tumbling habits
in and out of arms
and black blankets

The strange anatomies
of change blur
in sensation blur
in the mind's eye

How far if you think it
How near if not

Strange to say
getting over you
getting over the foibles
of a six day railroad ride

I can list a tin sun
summer din
silver sky entwining
old south tower
heaven's gate

You helped me carry the mind there
You led the way over borders
good Eurydice

Go first
Let the song carry
the mind's advance
towards the delight
of world

Good grass good bee balm good oleander
good horse good hoof good blade

Do not eat
among the dead

Spirit not food
Spirit the ghost
of food spilled in the path

As the bees do
we shed one another
advance through summer grass

Love the earth and the sun and the animals

Lt time wash the green hour
let it mend
the untorn
the untearable
the satisfaction
of our part
in the endless
world

Pain has its place
Regrets tremble in their place
Our places fine
Our places rooted in the mind
until they vanish as all things
vanish to be turned new

In the heart we build
our methods
and exchange them
leading the widower
following the hem of hell
from mind to world
tasting the fruit of strangers
full confident the song will pass over

Mountain meadow
neon orb
one hundred stories
nights and dawns

You write me
to say you
are moving to
the island

The sun
your skin
lovers and
uncertainties

A bicycle
ride
through
blooming
oranges

All I say
to you
love
is shining
in the brevity

MORNING

Gentleness is the hour when the birds come alive.
Cars in the street named after sunshine
hurry under the birds and the mercury willows
alive with the birds.
I am older
but I am learning the morning
light on the branches
late in its automatic evening
threshing dusk to the chirping
automatic dawn.
You go on to the sound
point where you will
give out and give the sole
last sound
my Master.
I am alive here in the dawn.

2002–2005

Thanks to Curtis Booth at Otis Nebula Press for making this book a book; to the folks at Otis Nebula; and to Peter Golub, Richard Cronshey, Sundin Richards, Michael McLane, Christopher Leibow, Ivana Gamarnik and Andrew Baron for their company in the trenches.

Poem to Get Started was a runner-up in the 2006 Utah Writers' Contest and was published in *Western Humanities Review*. Thanks to David McGlynn for his thoughtful editing there.

Thanks to George Haley, and Milton and Mirian Wadsworth, for years of generosity and council; and to the light of my life, Aurora Moore.

Finally thanks to Elena Suslov and Austin Booth, who came with.

www.ingramcontent.com/pod-product-compliance
Lightning Source LLC
Chambersburg PA
CBHW032150040426
42449CB00005B/460